Hope This Finds You Well

Poems by: Noble Gwyn

Dedicated to

To all my brothers whose lives didn't have fairy tale endings.
To all my lovers who never took the time to write these stories
with me. Hope this finds you well.

Eros

As an early morning sunrise,
Peaks over the cloud
So, do I rise
To peak over the majestic hills of her

Strong pressure awakens her.
Connected at the hip,
She grasps at air!
Melting into sheets; biting her lip.

Angels & Demons

Feeling sick to my stomach
Might be the combination of pills, NyQuil, coffee and
CranApple.
Sometimes I OD;
Just trying to be free.

My wifey just texted me
But I'm laid up with a mistress.
Adulterous!
Feeble man for hind quarters
Dime and quarters
Praying that gospel really changes

Its importance is evident,
Heaven sent, the son of God come to pay recompense.
So, why live like this?
Gotta funny feeling one day it'll come to a precipice!

Sword of wrath coming, am I ready?
White horse on a white cloud,
Fork in the road,

As I, straddle the fence!

Love

Because, the epitome of love
Is patience and kindness.
Not seeking its own selfishness!
Love protects hope and liberates trust,
It never fails.

Love exists;
In the form of warm words,
A soft touch,
Soothing to a weary soul!
So have you
Melted a polar heart?

Unity

To still fear that the past will haunt her until she can no longer
be hostage, catering to its worries and tears.
A newborn life smote in the hollowest part of her paunch and
a citadel of jeers.

Uniquely individual but equally indivisible as one. When one
suffers we all suffer and vice versa; when one rejoices we all
rejoice!

These markers that join the bonds of our path will forever
glow.

For heaven vouches for no one if they cannot testify to the
father's throne. So are you willing to hunt for me or live in the
past to blow away like chaff?

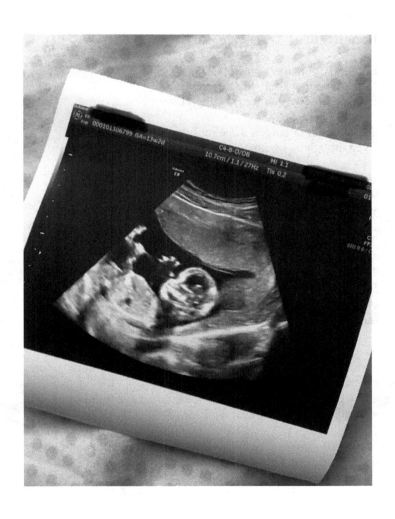

Beautiful Black Girl

Baby girl, you are beautiful!
Never let anyone tell you different;
Because, within you, lies the ingredients to life.

The strength to burden three jobs as a single parent,
Even though that wasn't your initial goal.

Taking care of your only child who suffers from chronic
illness but,
you still break your back to see him well!

That kind of love anchors the human heart!

To the belief that anything is possible;
Plowing into the soil of your soul, bringing forth the increase
of your bosom lingering in the air,
then residing on the barest of surfaces!

The pollination and flowering of hope released upon the earth,
connecting your spirit with that of the ones you've come into
contact, is like,
a bowl of shrimp étouffée and rice holding a wayfaring
stranger after a long day's work.

Much like you, as a beautiful woman, will hold down the ego
of boisterous man, whose, mindset can be
set on the trajectory of destruction.
You, Morgan Elise, are the epitome of beautiful.

And I've been praying something a little different for you!

One day you'll be able to look within
to see the attributes of a woman
And not look out into a sea of dead bodies
for approval from dead men!

Not focusing on hairstyles:

Angela Davis afros
Whoopi dreads or
Your mother's flat wrap.
They're all beautiful;
You're beautiful
And when I pray, I pray for you!

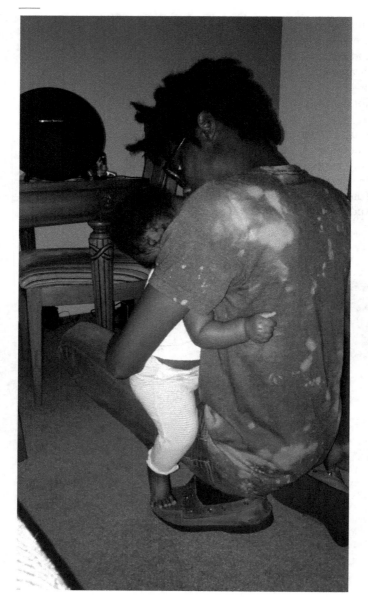

Crisis!

Writhing in pain, tortured!
None offered but praying for relief.
On the altar of myself,
I self-medicate thinking it'll help.

Transition

Hidden suggestion of intimacy but,
Hearts explore other arenas.
Having babies outside of legitimacy
And making his woman the love of my life.

This is just dream therapy
Of a drug induced kaleidoscope.
Rainbow colored tears full of apathy
I'm not sorry but hope there's hope for me.

Change and be better,
Sweaters and corduroy.
No longer, a caged gorilla or hyperactive stoner
But, a good ol' boy.

With the ability to love and care;
Key features obviously permanently attached.
I'm transparent and bare before your face,
This is not meant to be seen as weak.

Unrecognizable

Hey past,
I honestly didn't recognize you!
That's quite awkward because we've shared so many
incredible moments together.
However, there was this blood covering that disguised you
making you unrecognizable.
My apologies for not remembering those high times in the
laundry room at my mom's house
—or those occasions where me and someone's daughter
exchanged facial expressions in brief moments of passion.
I guess I did remember but I'm a long way from home.

All of life is

Who taught you to hate
our black skin?
This cold world did!

We were inkwells of pain;
writing stories
to never be forgotten.

Acts of love etch
our intimate scenes
onto hearts of stone,

That chose to see our
blackface as mere minstrelsy;
sneers to our striving.

Has our performance
ever been rose and
applause worthy?

Or has the house
lights been lowered on
our darkness?

Our hearts have been
a stage play into our lives.
Will you be our leading lady?

Opposite Existence

Someone once called me sun,
Well then, she must be the moon.
Because, as I radiate her days;
She illuminates my nights!
No longer blinded by darkness;
Yet, we can't exist together.

Soul Ties

I wish you would've taken my advice
When I told you that, you're weren't ready.
You probably didn't because you're too stubborn to admit that
I'm right!

Sadly, when that gun of premature relationship attempts goes
off,
Entering your heart, exploding, leaving shrapnel of soul-ties
everywhere,
As you bleed bitterness toward the opposite sex.

I'll wave from the side lines with compassion!

Wondering Wilderness

The heart draws near
To the warmth of a campfire.
The depths of her soul,
Desperately desire!

The crackle of twigs
Between the feet
Are, as loud as, the voices
That tells her to keep going.

Move faster wayfaring stranger;
Farther from the distant dim
Of cold lifeless gloom,
Closer to the lantern.

Closer to the light that attracts
The essence of her.
Every fiber of her being,
To the warmth of the burning light.

An incredible existence of air that whips around her face
as she gets the embrace of a new year.

In Time

When I die, is it too much to ask
That I'm remembered by my name.
Noble,
My words have power.

The ability to create change,
To uplift my community,
Touching the central part of a person and
Breathing life in their soul.

Mama named me noble
Seeing my necessity.
I whipped brothers with chains
In a time capsule of mental shackles.

Transatlantic Slave Trade mind,
Oppressive actions
Redefine my trajectory.
Who's next to me?

Just my name stands.

Black Rose

Much like a petite rose, delicate in nature, plucked from its
home soil,
Stuffed in a pot, wading the unnatural feeling of foreign dirt,
Surrounded by the presence of unfamiliarity,
Quiet hallelujahs quite hard to bring forth in this case.

This is government-sanctioned rape—the annihilation of
innocence that resides in our sisters.
Taken by a mister in return gifted a false image of beauty.

Beauty not as beautiful but useful!

A tool to pass the time,
Pollinating a deformed rose only spawns a deformed rose
bush!
We must cut it off at the root;
Reforming the deformed mindset of beauty.

Fight for your smile—the one on your face and the one
between your thighs.
Fight for your innocence.
Fight for your life.
Fight for your beauty.

Uhh

I never mind the sons of perdition;
Because, it's their constant position
to hate me and label everything
as hate speech.

Angels and demons together
Persuading the hearts of wayward men.
A bride and a lady in waiting,
Patiently groans to see her hope of new life.

Reminiscent

I remember playing with white keys,
Producing melodies that brought tears to the eyes of my
community.
A vicious cycle known all too well,

generational curses, come around like a needle on a
phonograph.
Scratching lives short of the crescendo.
Mahogany stained nightmares
String violin concerto of sorrow—
While no one cried for me.
The lyres never coax our souls to sleep
Only the reaper sung us lullabies.
As our mothers cried, "Not my baby!"

Don't Look

Catching plays with tears,
Can't see but can't drop the ball.
Streets are a mother's worst nightmare!
Don't look mama! I'm out here.

Dark places

No fear in my eyes.
Darkest of places I stand.
Watch evil quiver.
Avoiding faces,
Hiding tears,
As bodies shrivel!

Dear son:

A generation perishes and a generation is birthed.
Yet, we toil all the same—with sweat on our brow and
soreness in our shoulders.

We diminish humanity,
Where cultural barriers haven't fallen!
Walls that muffle King's speech;
We groan bitter despite his dream.

Men dig chasms in women's soul,
Missing her zenith,
Mortal flesh plundered,
Misdirected in what's going to make her come near.

Remnants with noble hearts.
Hearts that tremble at police sirens;
At the obtrusion of cultureless bullets
Mothers, daughters, and wives cry.

Oh, my dear son!

It's die or die trying;
Let's just rejoice we're making it.
The end is soon comes.
Yes, He soon comes!

3 am

Can't sleep,
Mind racing,
Confused,
With determination.

I love her;
Gucci Mane.
No candy lady,
My Coretta King.

Praise

Rising to the early morning worship songs of the birds,
He restlessly stumble to my knee to pray.
A sign of gratefulness!
Due only to his King of Kings.

At war with myself

I'm at war with myself,
Focused on making peace with myself but,
Deleting myself is the best option.
Question: "what about the people I'd fail?"

Untitled.

With love as the tone
He thought of texting, "I miss you!"
Envisioning them together, at last, kissing her.
But an emotional expanse between them is something
widespread.

Pick up and leave,
as though, they never really cared.
Forgetting those experiential releases
of endorphins they shared.

Disregarding their first love.
The reason they understand love isn't selfish or puffed
up.
The God that illuminates hearts and opens eyes,
will remove from their conversation so many "I've
been..!"

Finding their sanctification through the gospel;
Sober minded, righteously moving toward true
holiness!
Glorifying their father in heaven
Know this bread that brings life, cannot be spoiled
with a little leaven of
praise.

Rambling

Emotional graffiti litters,
Coffee stained pages,
My release from depression.
Heavy burdens are my cross,
Perhaps, I'm overreacting or—

grew up black!

Fence

In my defense
I'm still new at this
I have no defense
Against the elemental power of the air
The gospel is clear
Christ come to save mankind
Yet, I still fear.

I'm still trigger happy and lusty
But, I pray there's hope for me.

Justification

Heaven or hell?
Gimme both.
I'm entitled to it!

Marriage

Matrimony
Disagreements
Memorable moments
Discord

Protective order
Court appearances
Pregnancy
Covenants revived

Births
Separation
Bitterness
Sorrow

Mistress
Love
Moving on
Lost

I know I love you but I know we won't make it yet.

Feet shed

These frail bodies are not meant to just share
 the gospel in word but indeed as well!

Lord, help my feet to move in peace and my shield to be
strong in this war.

CPSIA information can be obtained
at www.ICGtesting.com
Printed in the USA
LVHW051659221121
704136LV00015B/2257